ILLUSTRATED SWIMMING, DIVING AND SURFING DICTIONARY FOR YOUNG PEOPLE

BY DIANA C. GLEASNER
ILLUSTRATED BY
STUART GOLDENBERG

HARVEY HOUSE
New York, New York

For Steve and Sue Gleasner

NOTE:

Since this dictionary defines terms for three slightly different water sports, we have identified which sport the definition refers to by using the following symbols:

 Swimming

 Diving

 Surfing

Copyright © 1980 by Harvey House, Publishers.

All rights reserved, including the rights
to reproduce this book or portions thereof in any form.
Manufactured in the United States of America.
ISBN 0-8178-0001-8
Library of Congress Catalog Card No. 79-93358

Harvey House, Publishers
20 Waterside Plaza, New York, New York 10010

Published in Canada by Fitzhenry & Whiteside, Ltd., Toronto

FOREWORD

Swimming is one of the world's oldest sports. Cave drawings done 11,000 years ago show people swimming. Ancient literature from many different parts of the world mention the sport. Thirty-six years before Christ was born, great competitions took place in Japan. However, organized swimming contests weren't held in the Western Hemisphere until the 1800s.

Once the contests started, the sport developed rapidly. Swimmers worked hard to improve their strokes so they would be able to win races.

The hand-over-hand stroke was brought to Europe in 1873 by John Trudgen, who had learned the style from the South American Indians. This was the beginning of the crawl stroke. The flutter kick was added in 1902 when an Australian used it in the International Championships. The stroke soon became known as the "Australian crawl." This powerful way of moving through water opened up new possibilities for speed.

Other strokes improved quickly as swimmers began competing. Before 1900, swimming on the back was more a stunt than an actual stroke. By 1912, the backstroke was recognized as a competitive event. The butterfly grew from the breaststroke. In the late 1950s, these two strokes were finally separated for competition.

Swimmers go through one of the most difficult conditioning programs in the world of sports. They must work hard. When they do, their bodies learn to adapt to extreme stress, becoming stronger and more efficient.

Pain is involved. Some swimmers refer to it as the "agony zone" that they must swim through. One coach said that compared with what his swimmers did in training, the workouts of professional football players were a joke.

The marathon or long-distance swimmer must meet the challenges of nature as well as other swimmers. It isn't easy. Marathon contests last at least five hours, so the swimmer must be strong. They often face frigid water, battle huge waves, and tangle with seaweed and jellyfish. They need a sense of adventure, great quantities of courage and, most important, the ability to hang in when the going gets tough.

It's satisfying to win races, break records, and receive awards. The ultimate triumph for a speed swimmer is to win a gold medal at the Olympics. But there are rewards throughout a swimmer's career.

Nothing compares with the great feeling of satisfaction that comes from setting a goal, working hard to achieve it, and then knowing the sweet taste of victory.

Of course swimming can be enjoyed strictly for recreation. Swimming is one of the few sports which the majority of people know how to perform with various degrees of competence. The Red Cross has successfully offered swimming and water safety instruction to millions of people.

Surfing began hundreds of years ago, probably in Polynesia. The sport was unknown to the western world until the islands of the Pacific Ocean were discovered. The English explorer Captain James Cook first described the art of surfing in one of the books he wrote about his voyages.

Riding ocean waves on a board was originally called the "sport of the kings" because in Hawaii only the chiefs were allowed to participate. Those early surfers had to be very strong since their giant hardcarved boards often weighed more than 150 pounds!

In 1819 young King Kamehameha II opened surfing to all Hawaiians when he did away with the rule that only members of the royalty could surf. But the missionaries who arrived from New England in 1920 were horrified because Hawaiians surfed in the nude and placed bets on the contests. Under missionary influence very little surfing was done for almost 100 years.

One of the few islanders who taught himself to surf in the early 1900s was Duke Kahanamoku. He and his friends started the first amateur surfing club at Waikiki Beach. They called their group *Hui Nalu* which means "Club of the Waves."

"The Duke," as he was affectionately known, became a champion Olympic swimmer and traveled all over the world to swimming competitions. Wherever there were waves to ride, he introduced surfing. Gradually the sport spread to the far corners of the earth.

Surfing got a big boost when Robert Simmons invented the modern surf board. Because it was made of polyurethane foam plastic covered with fiberglass, the Simmons board was very light and highly maneuverable.

The age of technology truly made the "sport of the kings" available to the common person. It wasn't too long before surfers carrying colorful mass-produced boards began to appear on beaches throughout the world whenever the surf was up.

Diving began in Europe as an outgrowth of tumbling and aerial acrobatics. In 1895 the Royal Life Saving Society of Great Britain held its first "graceful diving competition" and within a few years contests were being held in the United States. Those first dives were done from fixed platforms. Later when springboards were introduced, more difficult dives were invented. Diving became a highly developed form of gymnastics performed over water.

There are no "easy" ways to master the skills needed to be a champion diver. Divers put in hours and hours of practice.

Diving is considered an art as well as a challenging and spectacular sport. To perform well, divers must have excellent coordination, good balance, and exact timing. Perhaps most important is a keen sense of where their bodies are while they move through space. This awareness is what gives smoothness and grace to a diver's performance.

Just as important as physical ability is mental discipline. Every dive begins as an idea which is transformed into action upon leaving the springboard. This requires intense concentration. Divers must be very calm under pressure. In competition they only get one chance to perform each dive.

A

A.A.U. — Amateur Athletic Union, organization which supervises non-professional competitions in the U.S.A.

Advanced beginner — Red Cross classification given to someone who has mastered basic swimming and water safety skills with some degree of coordination and endurance.

Advanced swimmer — Red Cross classification given to a competent and versatile swimmer who has perfected all the swimming strokes.

Angle — to ride across the face of a wave either to the left or to the right, rather than straight ahead toward the beach.

Approach — the movement of the diver to the starting position for a dive.

Aquatics — sports which are practiced in or on the water such as swimming, diving, surfing, boating, etc.

Arm pull —  the movement of the arm through the water to propel the swimmer ahead.

Armstand dive —  a dive which begins in a handstand position at the end of the board or platform. The diver faces the board and falls away toward the water.

Australian crawl — a crawl in which the swimmer usually uses a two beat kick for each arm stroke. (see *Crawl.*)

B

Back crawl — 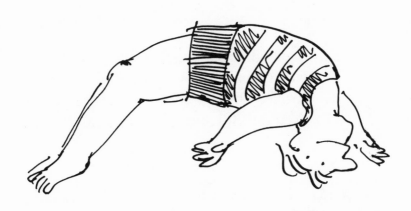 a swimming stroke performed on the back which combines a flutter kick with alternating arm pulls.

Back (or backward) dive — a dive which begins in a position facing the board or platform. The diver jumps and rotates backward to enter the water either feet first (facing toward the board) or head first (facing away from it).

Back flip — a back somersault performed in the air.

Back float — a floating position in which the swimmer lies on his back.

Back glide — a maneuver started either from pushing off a wall or after a leg stroke, which is performed in the back float position with arms at the swimmer's sides.

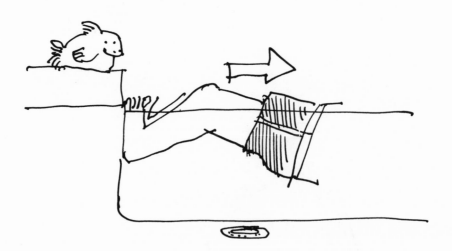

Backhand turn — ⌐ a left turn for a right-footed surfer; a right turn for a left-footed one.

Back header — ▷ a backward dive in which the diver enters the water head first.

Back jackknife — 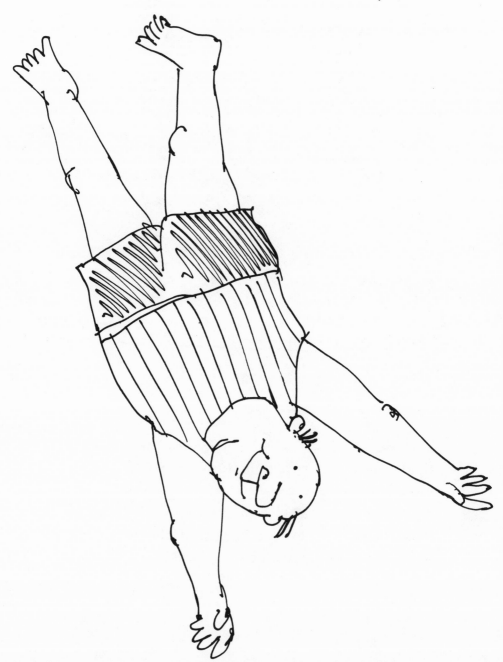 an inward dive done
in a jackknife position. (see *Jackknife.)*

Back off — a wave that begins to break but doesn't, and then forms itself anew.

Back one-and-a-half somersault — a backward somersault with an extra half revolution in which the diver enters the water head first.

Back out — to pull off a wave that could have been ridden.

Back (or backward) somersault — a dive which begins in a position facing the board. The diver completes a backward somersault before entering the water feet first.

Backstroke —  a swimming stroke performed on the back, usually either a back crawl or an elementary back stroke.

Back wash — water returning to the sea after a wave has broken on the shore.

Bail out — to jump or dive away from the surfboard to avoid a wipeout or possible collision.

Balsa wood — a very soft and light-weight wood used for surfboard construction in the 1940s and 1950s.

Barge — a large, heavy surfboard.

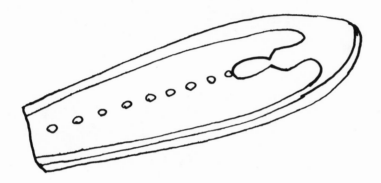

Beach break — a wave that breaks on or near a sandy beach rather than on a reef or point.

Beat — the number of leg kicks to a cycle of arm strokes.

Beginner — Red Cross classification given to someone who has mastered basic swimming and water safety skills.

Belly — underside or bottom of a surfboard.

Belly board — a small, short surfboard usually used with swim fins while surfing in a prone position.

Belly flop — a fall or dive in which the front of the diver's body slaps against the water first. Also called "belly whopper."

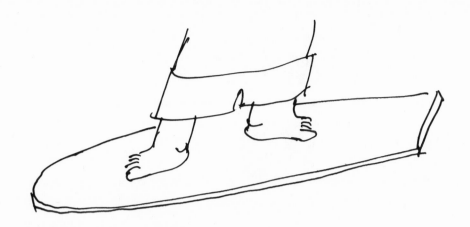

Bicycle —  to ride a surfboard with legs apart.

Big daddy — a huge breaker.

Big gun — a large surfboard designed for heavy surf.

Bobbing — the act of alternately submerging under the water and rising above its surface for air, usually in a vertical position.

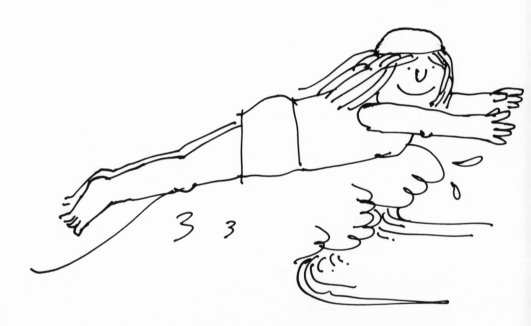

Body surfing — a sport in which a surfer uses only his/her body to ride the waves without help of a board of any other flotation device.

Boomer —  a huge wave too large to be ridden.

Bottom turn — a turn made at the base of a wave's face.

Bounce — lifting the surfboard's nose from the water by shifting weight and then letting it fall back.

Bowl —  a shallow area which causes waves to break harder and faster than usual.

Break — the point at which a wave peaks and its crest collapses.

Breaker — any wave that collapses on its way to the shore.

Breaststroke — a swimming stroke done in the prone position which combines the frog or whip kick, a glide with arms stretched over the head and an underwater double arm pull outward and rearward.

Bumps —  lumps or thickened patches of skin on a surfer's knees and/or tops of feet caused by continual paddling. Also called "knots."

Butterfly stoke — a swimming stroke done in the prone position which combines a dolphin kick and a double overarm pull. When the arms come together over the head, they resemble butterfly wings. (see *Dolphin kick.)*

C

Cannonball — a feet first jump into the water done in a curled-up position with the arms holding the knees closely against the chest. Usually used to make a big splash.

Catalyst — 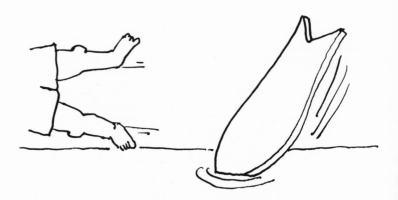 a chemical that causes the plastic resins used in making surfboards to harden or soften faster.

Catch a rail — to dig an edge of the surfboard into the water resulting in a wipe-out.

Chip — a Simmons board or any of the earlier balsa wood boards that were considerably smaller than the large redwood boards originally used in surfing.

Choppy — bouncy little waves caused by wind ruffling the surface water.

Close-out — ⟋ big waves that can't be ridden because they break all at once instead of from one side to the other.

Coffin — ⟋ a novelty position in which the surfer lies on his/her back on the board with feet extended and arms crossed.

Comber — ⟋ a large, curling wave.

Compulsory dive — a dive which must
be performed by all divers participating in a
particular competition.

Crasher — a powerful wave which
breaks heavily from top to bottom.

Crawl — 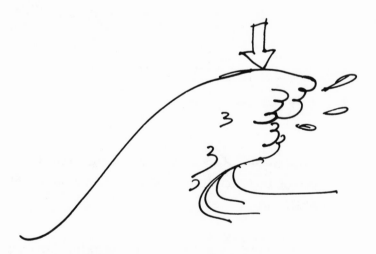 a swimming stroke done in the prone position which combines a flutter kick with alternate overarm pulls. The fastest and most popular stroke for freestyle competition.

Crest — the topmost part of the wave before it breaks.

Critical — steep and extremely challenging wave or portion of the wave.

"Cross" position — position in which the arms are held perpendicular to the shoulders. Also called "T" position.

Crouch — the squatting position a surfer uses to duck under the spilling crest of the wave.

Curl — the curved breaking portion of a wave between the face of the wave and its spilling crest.

Custom board — 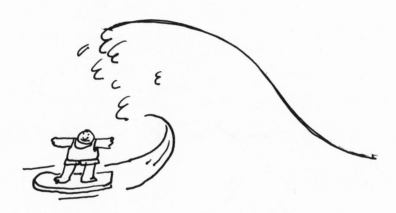 a board tailor-made for an individual.

Cutaway — see *Inward dive.*

Cut back — to turn back toward the breaking part of the wave.

Cut out — to end a ride by pulling out of a wave.

Cut the board — leaving the board too soon before getting the greatest possible spring.

D

Deadman's float — a prone floating position in which the arms are stretched forward and the legs extended backward. Also called "prone float" or "survival float" because to breathe, all you have to do is raise your head.

Deck — top surface of the surfboard.

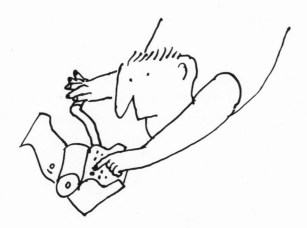

Degree of difficulty — a dive's numerical rating based on its difficulty. Dives are rated according to body position and the height of the board from which the dive begins. The higher the number, the greater is the dive's degree of difficulty.

Dig — to paddle forcefully.

Dig a rail — to catch the edge of the surfboard in the water.

Ding — a chip or dent in the skin of the surfboard.

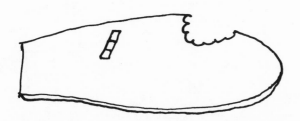

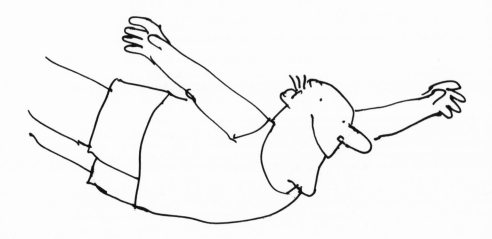

Diving — 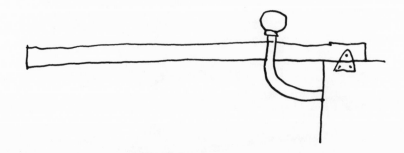 a highly specialized aquatic sport that involves a plunge into water in a prescribed way, usually from a diving board or platform.

Diving board — a flexible board extending over the water. For competitive diving, the boards are mounted one to three meters above the water. Also called "springboard."

Diving judge —  one who evaluates and scores the divers' form in competition.

Diving well — the area of a swimming pool under the diving boards and/or platforms which is deep enough that divers do not hit bottom after entering the water.

Dog paddle — 🎵 a simple swimming stroke done in a prone position with head out of the water, legs kicking and arms paddling underwater.

Dolphin kick — 🎵 a kick used with the butterfly stroke in which the legs stay together while moving up and down, and the knees bend slightly on the upward movement. The legs' motion resembles the way a dolphin moves its body when it swims.

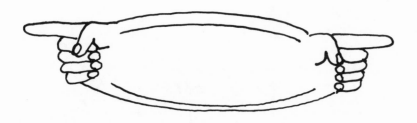

Double ender —  a surfboard shaped the same on both ends.

Down — quiet surf. (see *Flat.*)

Driving — an extra effort made to gain the greatest speed.

Drop in — to slide down the steepest section of the wave just after catching it.

Drop-off — ⌒ a sudden deepening of water.

Dump — ⌒ to wipe out.

Dumper — ⌒ a large wave which suddenly collapses.

E

Ebb tide — ⌒ the outgoing tide returning to the sea.(see *Flood tide.*)

Elementary back stroke — 🏊 a swimming stroke combining an inverted frog or whip kick with a double arm pull which is performed on the back.

Entry — the point at which the diver enters the water, head first or feet first, at the completion of a dive. Divers try to achieve a smooth, clean entry without making much splash.

Eskimo roll — a maneuver in which the surfer passes through an oncoming wave by wrapping legs around the board and rolling over so he/she is on the bottom.

Execute — perform or do.

F

Face —  the unbroken front surface of a wave between the crest and the trough.

Fade — a maneuver in which the surfer turns back toward the curl in order to prolong his ride.

Fancy diving —  formal name for competitive diving.

Fathom — a measurement of water equal to six feet.

Feathering wave — a wave just beginning to break or with only the top portion breaking.

Fetch — the uninterrupted distance traveled by wind where surfing swells are created.

Fiberglass — a material woven from fine glass filaments which is used in modern surfboard construction.

Fin — a fixed rudder or skeg attached to the rear bottom of the surfboard to stabilize it.

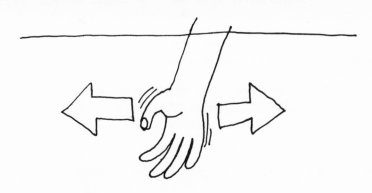

Fin — to move hands back and forth through the water.

F.I.N.A. — Federation International Natation Association. The organization in charge of guidelines for swimming and diving competitions held in the Olympics.

Fin box — a box at the rear bottom of the surfboard in which the fin is anchored.

Fins — a pair of rubber flippers worn on the feet, often used in body surfing. Also called "swim fins."

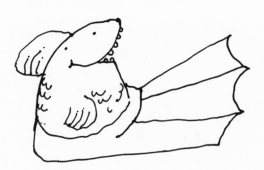

Flat — 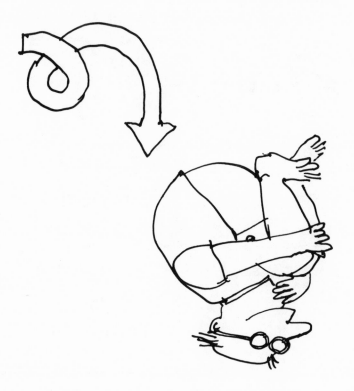 calm conditions; no surf.

Flip — a somersault performed in the air.

Flip turn — 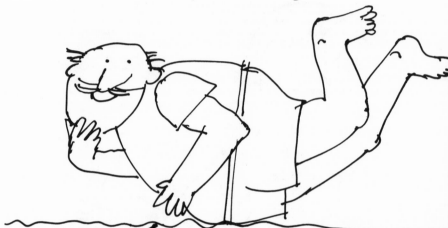 a racer's turn at the end of the pool. The swimmer does a half forward somersault and half twist under water, then pushes off the wall with the feet. Flip turns are the fastest way to turn during a race.

Float — to rest buoyantly at the surface of the water.

Flood tide — the incoming or rising tide. Opposite of ebb tide.

Flutter board — see *Kick board*.

Flutter kick — a kick from the hip in which the legs move alternately up and down as in the crawl and back crawl; knees are usually straight, but flexible.

46

Foam —  the frothy mixture of air and water on the surface of the ocean caused by breaking waves. Also called "white water" or "soup."

Forward dive — a dive which begins in a position facing away from the diving board. The diver enters the water either head first facing the board or feet first facing away from it.

Free — short for "freestyle."

Free fall — a fall from the top of a steep wave.

Free position —  a diver's choice of diving positions including one or more of the basic pike, layout, and tuck positions.

Freestyle — competition in which each swimmer may choose any stroke. Often freestyle is used to mean crawl stroke because the crawl is invariably used in freestyle races since it's the fastest.

Frog kick — a kick in which the legs are bent at the knees, extended outward and quickly pulled together. Primarily used in the breaststroke and elementary backstroke. This kick resembles the leg movements of swimming frogs.

Front dive — see *Forward dive.*

Front header —  a forward dive, often involving one or more somersaults, in which the diver enters the water head first.

Fulcrum — the support or point on which a diving board rests. One end of the board is anchored, the other is free to bounce upon. If the diver wants more spring, the fulcrum is moved back toward the anchored end.

Full — a complete twist or somersault.

G

Gainer —  see *Reverse dive.*

Glass — short for "fiberglass."

Glass off — to have the ocean surface flatten when the winds die.

Glassy — smooth ocean surface un-ruffled by wind.

Goofy-foot — a position in which the surfer rides with his right foot forward.

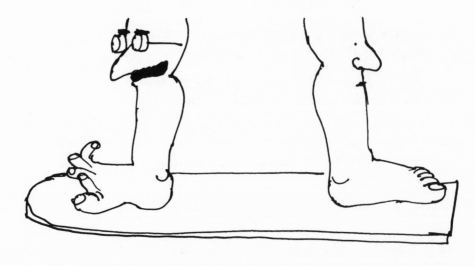

Grab the rail —  to pull out of a wave by taking hold of the edge of the board on the side opposite the wave's crest and pulling the front of the board around.

Gremmie — a beginning surfer. Also called "gremlin."

Ground swell — 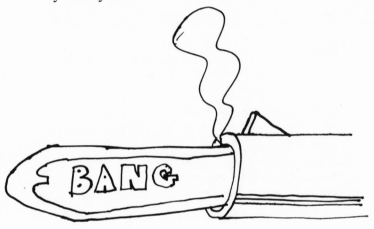 an unbroken wave that has traveled a great distance from where it began.

Gun — a long surfboard designed for very heavy surf.

H

Hang five — to move forward on the surfboard and place five toes of one foot clearly over the edge of the nose.

Hang heels — to place the heels over the surfboard's edge while riding facing backward.

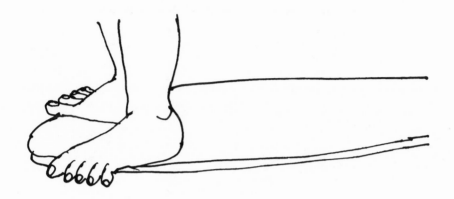

Hang ten — to move forward on the surfboard and ride with all ten toes clearly draped over the nose of the board.

Head dip — a maneuver performed while surfing by lowering the head and dipping it into the wall of the wave.

Heavy (or heavies) — very large surf.

High board — a diving board three meters above the water.

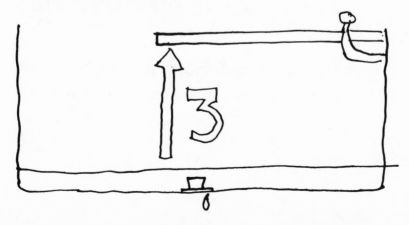

Hip lift —  a movement in which a diver elevates his/her hips on taking off from the diving board.

Hold the rail — grab the edge of the board to stay balanced.

Hollow — the concave, deeply curling face of the wave.

Honing — perfectly formed waves that break cleanly and evenly; ideal conditions for surfing.

54

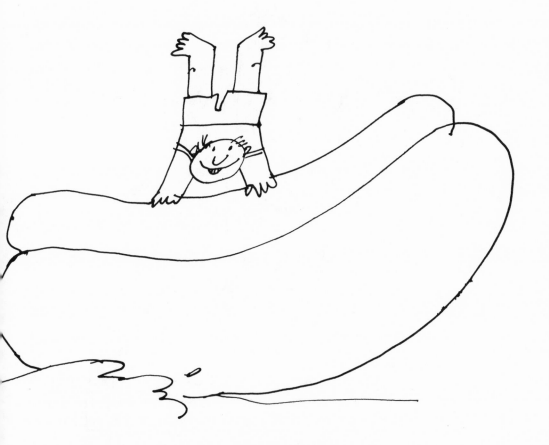

Hot dog — to maneuver quickly on a wave performing stunts and demonstrating great agility while riding.

Hump —  a mound-shaped unbroken swell.

Hurdle — the short leap or spring usually made on the last step of a diver's approach.

I

I.A.S.F. —  International Amateur Surfing Federation.

Individual medley — a race in which each competitor must swim each leg with a different prescribed stroke. The usual order is: butterfly, backstroke, breaststroke, and front crawl.

Inshore —  the shoal water on the beach side of the break.

Inside — the area between the shoreline and the outside line of breaking waves.

Inside break — the wave which breaks nearest the beach.

Intermediate swimmer — Red Cross classification given to someone who has mastered basic swimming strokes and rescue skills.

Inward dive — a dive which begins from a position facing the diving board. The diver jumps up and out from the board but rotates forward toward the board. Entry may be either head or feet first.

J

Jackknife — a forward dive in pike position. The diver bends in midair to touch the toes and then immediately straightens out before entering the water head first. In the air, the diver's body resembles a "pocket knife" or "jackknife."

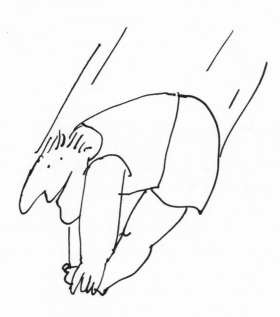

Jellyfish float —  a prone float in a tuck position or with legs and arms hanging downward.

K

Kick — the propelling movement of the feet and legs as they move up and down or back and forth through the water.

Kickboard — a buoyant board used to support the upper body while practicing kicking. Also called "flutterboard."

Kick out — an abrupt turn up and over the crest of the wave to end a ride.

Kick stall —  a maneuver performed on longer boards in which the surfer stands at the back of the board and kicks it to a vertical position which momentarily halts its forward movement, then immediately retrims and continues riding. (see *Stalling.*)

Knots — see *Bumps.*

L

Lane — 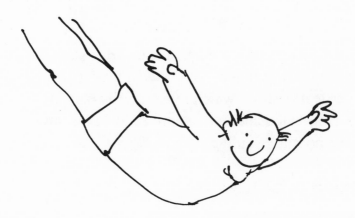 a marked-off course in a swimming pool within which a competitor must remain during a race.

Lap — one length of a pool.

Layout — a position in diving in which the body is extended, the legs together and straight and arms are either parallel overhead or stretched out to the sides.

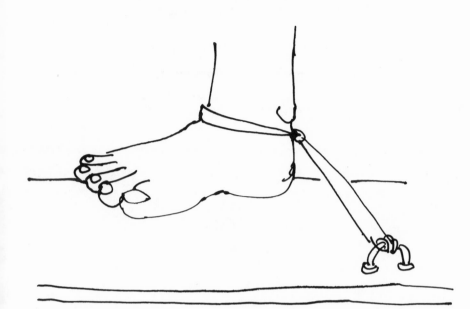

Leash — a cord attached to the surfboard at the skeg which is tied to the surfer's ankle, so the surfer doesn't lose the board after a spill.

Left — a wave that breaks from left to right as a surfer stands on the beach watching it.

Left slide — to ride across the face of a wave to the left when facing toward the shore.

Leg — the part of a course which each member of a relay team must cover.

Line-up —   a gathering of surfers at a point in the ocean where waves are breaking consistently.

Lip — the thin crest of a hollow wave just starting to break.

Locked in — sliding in the curl of a wave which is closing.

Long course — a pool or open course which is fifty meters or fifty-five yards long.

Looper — a large wave that breaks over the surfer putting him/her inside the curl.

Low board — a diving board one meter above the water.

M

Marathon —  a long distance swimming race, usually eighteen miles.

Mark —  position taken by a swimmer at the starting block immediately prior to the signal that begins a race.

Medley — a relay race in which each team member must swim a different stroke.

Meet — an athletic competition between two or more teams.

Milk a wave — get the longest ride from a wave that is possible.

Mush (or mushy) — slow, sloppy waves that break and die quickly.

N

Natation —  the act or sport of swimming.

Natatorium — a swimming pool, usually indoors.

Noncontact sport — a sport such as swimming, diving, and surfing in which individuals compete but don't try to hinder their opponents or have physical contact with them.

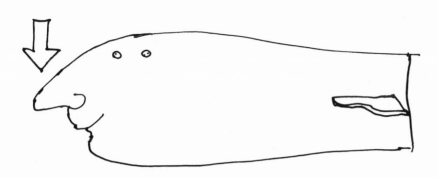

Nose –  front end of surfboard.

Novice – a beginner or a competitor who has not been a winner in a particular event.

O

Offshore wind – a wind blowing away from the land toward the sea.

Olympic-sized pool – a swimming pool fifty meters long.

One-and-a-half somersault — a dive consisting of a full somersault with an additional half turn which enables the diver to enter the water head first.

One meter board — a diving board one meter above the water. Also called "low board."

Onshore wind — a wind blowing from the ocean toward the land.

Optional dive —  a dive, usually in competition, which is the diver's choice as opposed to a compulsory dive which is required. The diver usually chooses a dive he/she does especially well.

Outside —  the seaward side of the breaking waves.

Over the falls — getting caught on top of a breaking wave and being poured over the curl.

Overarm — performed with arm(s) lifted from the water and reaching beyond the head on recovery. The front and back crawl and the butterfly use overarm strokes.

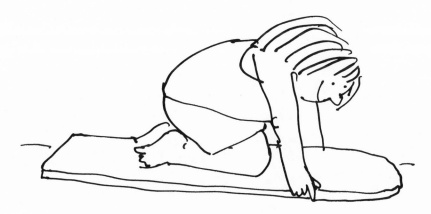

P

Paddle – 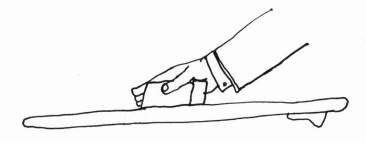 to pull arms and hands through the water to move surfboard.

Paddling out – using arm strokes while kneeling or lying prone on the board, the surfer moves seaward to a good position for catching waves.

Paraffin – wax used on deck of surfboard to make it less slippery.

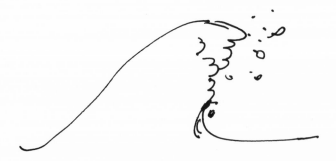

Peak —  the very top of the wave before breaking.

Pearl — to catch the nose of the board resulting in a wipeout. The term comes from pearl diving.

Peeler — a wave that curls evenly and quickly without breaking ahead of itself.

Peeling — breaking evenly across the face of the wave.

Pig (or pig board) — a short surfboard widely rounded at the rear.

Pike — a position in diving in which the body is bent or flexed at the hips and the knees are straight.

Pipe — a wave which has curled over on itself creating a hollow. Also called "a tube."

Platform — a flat surface from which dives are performed. For national and international competition, the platform is ten meters above the water. Also called *tower.*

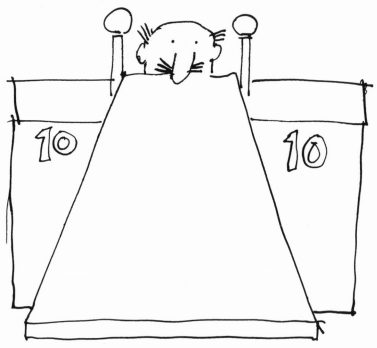

Point break — breakers caused by a pier, jetty, or point of land jutting into the sea.

Points — individual swimmers receive points based on how they placed in each race. These are totaled to determine the overall team standings.

Points — divers are judged on the execution of a dive including approach, take-off, movements in the air, and water entry. Points for diving style are adjusted by a degree of difficulty factor for each dive.

Pool —  a large artificial basin filled with water for swimming. Standard size pools for competition are 25 yards or 25 meters (short course) and 55 yards or 50 meters (long course.)

Prone float — a face down floating position. (see *Deadman's float.*)

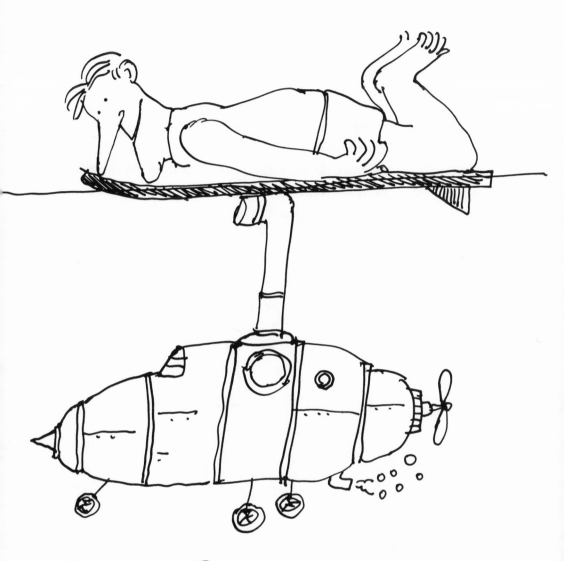

Prone out — ⟑ to lie face down on the surfboard.

Pull — 🏊 the part of a stroke in which the hand and arm move through the water to propel the swimmer ahead.

Q

Quadrangle meet —  a meet scored as if each of four teams were simultaneously competing against each of the other teams. Individual member's points are totaled to get the team score and the team with the highest number of points is credited with three victories.

Quiver — a selection of two or more boards designed for various wave conditions.

R

Racing dive — a flat shallow dive used at the start of a crawl, breaststroke or butterfly race or a leg of a relay race. (Backstroke races start with the swimmers in the water.) The idea behind a racing dive is to land as flat on the surface as possible so you can start swimming as soon as possible.

Rail —  side or edge of surfboard.

Rail turn — to turn while the edge of the board is locked into the wave.

Recall — the calling back of swimmers just after the starting gun because of a false start.

Recovery — 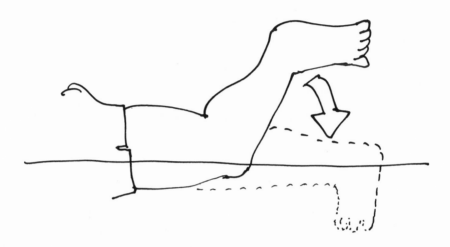 the motion of an arm or leg being returned to its original position.

Reef — 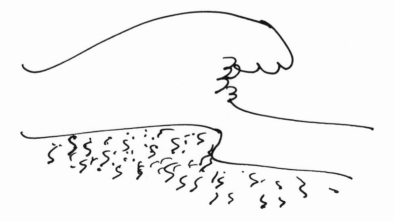 a ridge of rock, sand, or coral at or near the surface of the water which causes waves to peak and break.

Reentry —  a maneuver to bypass a wave's breaking section and reenter the smooth part. The surfer rides to the top of the wave and across the curl, then down the face of the wave.

Referee — the official in charge of a competition.

Relay — a race between teams in which only one team member competes at a time and different individuals compete on each leg of the race.

Resin — a plastic liquid adhesive used to bind fiberglass to a foam base in surfboard construction.

Reverse dive — a dive which begins in a position facing away from the diving board. The diver springs up and rotates backward to enter the water either head first facing the board or feet first facing away from the board.

Reverse takeoff —  a skeg-first takeoff. After catching a wave, the surfer simultaneously stands and rotates his board 180 degrees to a standard takeoff position.

Right slide — to ride across the face of a wave to the right when facing toward shore.

Rip — a strong, often turbulent, current of water returning to sea.

Rogue — a wave unlike the preceding waves which appears suddenly and without warning.

Roller coaster — ⌒ to ride up the steep face of the wave and angle down off the lip.

Roll over —  a paddling-out maneuver used in heavy surf in which a surfer rolls his board bottom side up and hangs on underneath while the wave passes over. Also called "eskimo roll."

Rotation — a turning around as on an axis, or in a spin.

S

Sandbar — 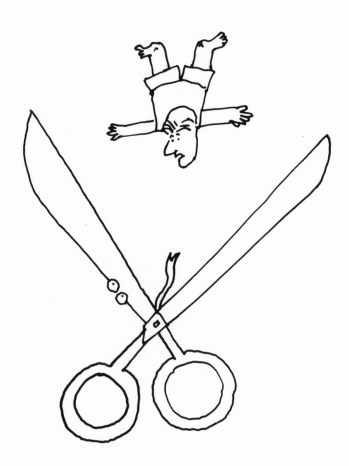 a build-up of sand formed by ocean currents.

Scissors kick — the kick usually used in the side stroke in which the legs are separated and brought together in a movement resembling scissors blades.

Scorecard — cards with number scores exhibited by judges shortly after each diver performs. The scores range up to "10".

Sectioning — a wave breaking in two or more places at once rather than breaking evenly across its face from one side to the other.

Set —  a group of three to six waves rolling shoreward in succession.

Shoal — shallow water usually caused by a reef or sandbar.

Shoot the curl — to ride inside the hollow part of a wave's curl. Also called "shoot the tube."

Shore break —  waves that break close to the beach.

Short course — a course 25 yards or 25 meters in length.

Shoulder — the unbroken portion of a wave sloping away from the curl.

Shuffle — a maneuver in which a surfer moves toward the nose of the board by sliding his feet along the deck.

Sideslipping — 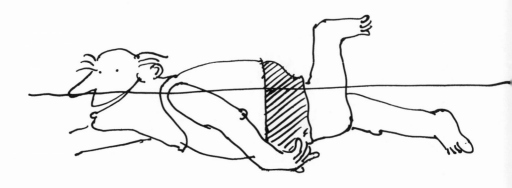 the controlled release of the rail or skeg from the wave resulting in the board sliding sideways.

Sidestroke — a stroke done with the swimmer on his/her side which combines a scissors kick with an alternate underwater arm pull.

Simmons board — the contemporary board, invented by Robert Simmons, made of polyurethane foam covered with fiberglass sealed with plastic resins.

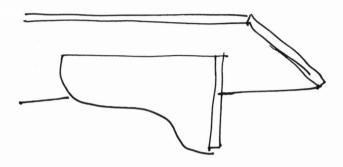

Skeg — the fin or rudder attached to the rear underside of the surfboard for stability.

Slide — to ride across the face of the wave roughly parallel to the shore either to the left or the right.

Slot — a surfer's ideal position in the wave.

Snuff out —  a sudden wipeout.

Somersault — a complete revolution of the body, either backward or forward, with a feet first entry into the water.

96

Soup —  the foamy white water made by a breaking wave.

Spinner — a maneuver in which the surfer and board both spin 360 degrees and end up facing in the same direction that they started on the wave.

Springboard — see *Diving board.*

Sprint — a short race performed at maximum speed, usually 100 yards or 100 meters or less.

Stalling — slowing or stopping the surfboard by shifting weight toward the tail and lifting the nose. (see *Kick stall.*)

Starter — one who starts in a race, or the person who gives the signal (usually by firing a pistol) to competitors to begin a race.

Starting block — a low platform at one end of the pool where the competitor stands for the start of a race or leg of a relay.

Step-off — measuring the strides of a diver's approach so as to determine the exact point of takeoff.

Stick — slang for "surfboard."

Stoked — slang for "excited."

Stringer — a narrow strip of wood that runs down the longitudinal centerline of many surfboards adding strength and stiffness.

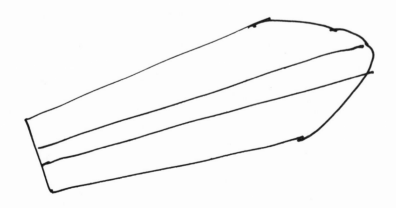

Stroke — a type or method of swimming which combines distinctive arm and leg movements. Also, the propelling push or pull of the arms or legs.

Submarine — a surfboard too small for the surfer.

Surf — the breaking swell of the sea, usually on or near the shore.

Surfing —  the sport of riding the waves. In competition, surfers must ride a specified number of waves in a certain time period and are judged on the length of the ride and their maneuvering ability on the wave.

HOW TO SURF

Surface dive — 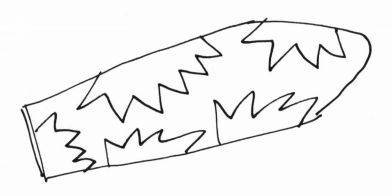 a dive, either head or feet first, made from the surface of the water.

Surfboard — a narrow board used for riding the waves.

Surf-off — the final round in competition.

Surf's down — poor surfing conditions; no ridable waves.

Surf's up — excellent surfing conditions created by breaking waves.

Swan dive — a forward dive in layout position with arms outstretched at shoulder height before water entry with arms stretched above the head.

Swell — 〽 an unbroken wave or series of unbroken waves.

Swimmer — 🏊 Red Cross classification given to someone who has perfected most of the swimming strokes and rescue skills.

Swimmer — 🏊 someone who has mastered the ability to move through the water; someone who swims.

Swimming — 🏊 moving through the water by coordinating leg and arm action.

Switchfoot — 〽 a surfer who can surf with either foot forward.

T

"T" position — 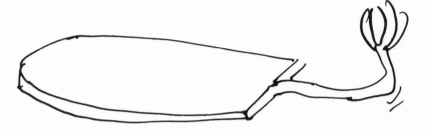 see *Cross*.

Tail — rear end of surfboard.

Takeoff — the point at which a diver leaves the surface of the board or platform.

Tandem — two surfers riding together on one board.

Tank suit —  a lightweight skin-tight suit worn in swimming and diving competition.

Ten-point dive —  the highest possible score in competition.

Three meter board — a diving board or platform three meters above the water. Also called "high board."

Toes over — hanging some or all of a surfer's toes over the nose of the board.

Tower — see *Platform.*

Tracking — the surfboard's tendency to go straight ahead.

Trail arm – the arm the surfer extends behind while riding a wave.

Trail leg – the foot nearest the rear of the surfboard.

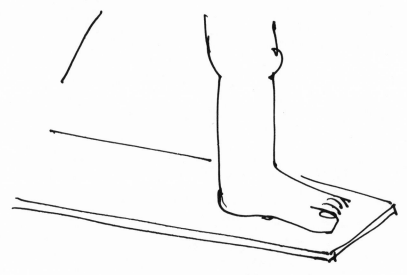

Trash – frothy, unridable waves.

Treading water —  maintaining the body in a vertical position in the water with the head above the surface by moving the arms and legs.

Trim — to distribute a surfer's weight on the board to achieve the best planing angle.

Trough — the lowest point between two waves.

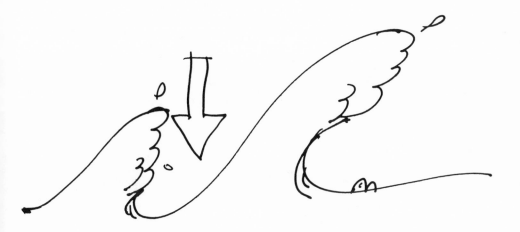

Trudgen stroke —  a stroke done in the prone position which combines a crawl arm motion and a scissors kick. Named for the British swimmer, John Arthur Trudgen, who made it popular.

Tube — a hollow tunnel formed by the curl of the wave.

Tuck —  a position in which the body is rolled up in a ball with the knees drawn close to the chest.

ARF
ARF

Turn — a swimmer's method of reversing direction at the end of the pool. (see *Flip turn.*)

Twist — a dive which involves a rotation around the body's vertical axis.

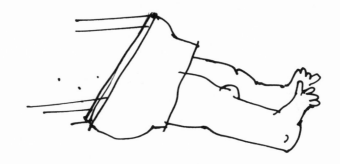

U

Undertow — a current flowing seaward beneath the surface of the water.

U.S.S.A. — United States Surfing Association.

U.S.S.F. — United States Surfing Foundation.

W

Wax — coating applied to the deck of a surfboard to provide firm footing.

Wet suit — a neoprene foam suit which keeps a surfer warm in cold water by allowing a layer of water next to the skin which becomes heated by body temperature. Also used by scuba divers.

Whip kick — 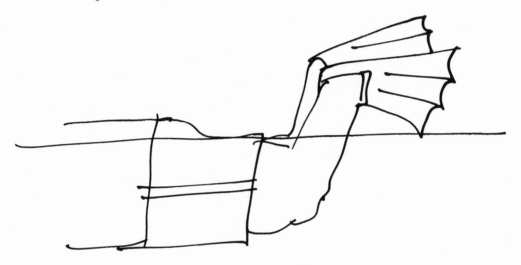 a modified version of the frog kick done with the legs closer together. Primarily used with the breaststroke in competition.

White water — the foamy part of a breaking wave.

Wind waves — waves created by the wind.

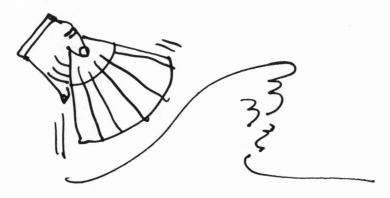

Wipeout — a fall from the surfboard resulting from loss of control.

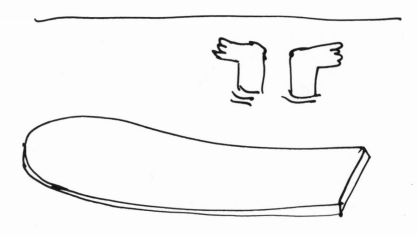

Z

Zigzag –  a surfing maneuver in which direction on the wave is changed several times.

Duke Kahanamoku is the father of modern surfing. He was born in 1890 to a royal family in Hawaii. At four he started surfing at Waikiki, the famous beach on the island of Oahu. Surfers used big heavy boards in those days, and youngsters taught themselves to ride the waves.

Duke was a strong, fast swimmer used to battling ocean currents. This great swimming ability brought him fame and made his name known around the globe. He shattered a number of world records in freestyle swimming events and was an Olympic athlete in the sport for twenty years. Whenever he traveled to compete in swim meets, Duke promoted surfing. He gave demonstrations and taught others the pleasures of wave riding. His enthusiasm and superb athletic ability made him loved and respected wherever he went.

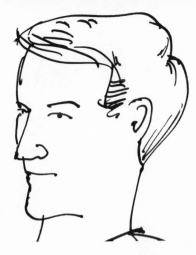

In Italy his fellow countrymen call *Klaus Dibiasi* the "Blond Angel." The name fits. When he dives from a platform which is as high as a four-story building, Klaus seems to have wings. Also, he is a gentle man who has always been gracious toward his competitors and modest about his accomplishments.

Dibiasi's angelic nature contains a core of courage. After he was defeated at the 1964 Olympic Games, the painfully shy 17-year-old dedicated himself to becoming champion diver of the world. With the help of his father who was also his coach, Klaus put in years of training to perfect his skills.

Hard work paid off. His grace, consistency, and control earned him gold medals at the Olympic Games in Mexico, Munich, and Montreal. He almost withdrew from the Montreal Games because of an extremely sore ankle tendon. The crowd was treated to a spectacular demonstration of Dibiasi's diving feats when he decided to ignore the pain and give it a try.

Diana Nyad wanted more than anything else in the world to win a gold medal for swimming in the Olympics. She trained for it from the time she was in elementary school, but serious illness stopped her. However, nothing could take away her drive to excel. She decided to try marathon swimming after her coach told her each race would be an adventure.

She soon found out that adventure meant avoiding sharks and rocky coasts, fighting riptides and outswimming incredibly strong men. Some races started in the afternoon and didn't end until the *next* afternoon. She endured bleeding eyes, periods of unconsciousness and rushed trips to the hospital.

122

Diana thinks it's worth it. "I really believe I can do anything I set my mind to," she says. "It takes a lot of guts to attempt, much less survive, this sport. The work and pain going into it are extremely demanding, but the satisfaction is very rewarding."

Diana has been women's overall long-distance champion and holds many marathon records including a 28-mile swim around Manhattan in less than eight hours. She has swum 67 miles in the North Sea, 50 miles from the Great Barrier Reef to Australia, and was the first person to swim from the Bahamas to Florida — a 60-mile feat that took 27 hours and 38 minutes.

Margo Oberg has said, "I want to be the first woman to ride 30-foot surf."

This small blonde spunky Californian won her first contest at the age of 12 when she soundly beat all fifty boys in her age division. She liked winning so the next year she returned and took first place again. A string of victories on the California circuit

123

earned her a berth on the team going to the 1968 world contest in Puerto Rico. Fifteen-year-old Margo Godfrey returned home having the title of Woman's Champion of the World.

After high school Margo moved to Hawaii where she married fellow surfer Steve Oberg. At 18, she had won all the amateur titles she cared about. Since there didn't seem to be any future for a woman in surfing, she settled down to a domestic life.

As soon as women's surfing competition began to grow and a professional circuit was started, the former world champion came out of retirement. At 22 Margo wanted to know if she could still compete.

Her many years of experience paid off. She enjoyed a decisive victory at Malibu in the first pro surfing contest ever held for women. Since that time Margo has won many international competitions. She has also been in surfing movies, done commercials and appeared on a number of television programs.

Margo plans to surf the rest of her life and, like most surfers, she's always on the lookout for the ultimate wave. If she gets her wish, it'll be 30 feet high!

Mark Spitz started swimming when he was eight years old. By the time he was ten he was swimming for an hour and a half every day. That year he set his first United States record. His father said he wasn't interested in seeing Mark win age group races. He told his son to go after world records. Mr. Spitz said, "Swimming isn't everything. Winning is."

1967 was a good year for Mark. He broke five world records, earned five gold medals in the Pan-American games and was named Swimmer of the Year by *Swimming World* magazine. But at the 1968 Mexico Olympics he didn't win a single individual race.

Four years later at the 1972 Olympic Games in Munich, Mark Spitz made a spectacular comeback. The 22-year-old Californian won seven gold medals. He is the first athlete to ever win more than five gold medals in one Olympiad. Mark set seven world records winning the 100-meter and 200-meter freestyle races, the 100-meter and 200-meter butterfly events and swimming on the winning 400-meter and 800-meter freestyle and the 400-meter relay teams.

Mark Spitz is a name that will live forever in swimming history.

Maxine Joyce King, better known as *Micki,* started diving when she was ten. Her mother wanted her to become a figure skater, but Micki found the routine boring. She won her first diving meet at 15 but admits she was far from being an expert. "I didn't even know the names of the dives I did," she said.

What she did know was that she loved the sport. Micki first tried platform diving at the end of her freshman year at The University of Michigan. Knowing that a diver hits the water at about 40 miles an hour from that height was scary. Sometimes she hit with such force her shoulders and upper arms turned black and blue.

Micki King overcame her fear and went on to be the first woman ever to do a back 1½ somersault with 2½ twists off the tower. She also was the first to do the reverse 1½ somersault with 2½ twists from the springboard.

At the Mexico Games in 1968, she was in the lead when she hit the board with a sickening thud. Her arm was broken and her chance for a medal shattered. Micki made up for her mistake four years later at the Munich Olympics when she finally earned her gold medal.

Since Micki always wanted more out of life than a routine job, she joined the Air Force in 1966. Today Captain Micki King is held in high esteem by the cadets of the U.S. Air Force Academy where she teaches and coaches diving.